ICELAND

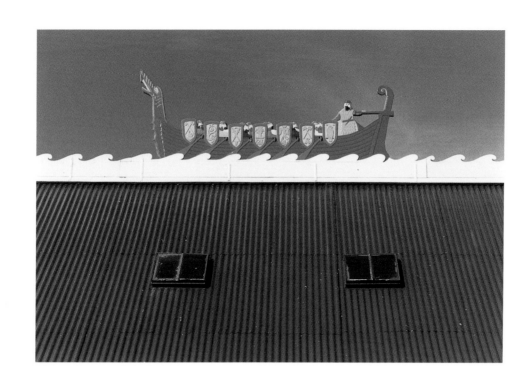

First published in Great Britain in 2001 by
Colin Baxter Photography Ltd.
Grantown-on-Spey, PH26 3NA, Scotland

www.colinbaxter.co.uk

Photographs copyright © Colin Baxter 2001
Text by Cathy Harlow, copyright © Colin Baxter Photography 2001
All rights reserved

A CIP catalogue record for this book is available from the British Library

ISBN 1-84107-071-8

Printed in Hong Kong

Front Cover Photograph: Öræfajökull, Hrútsfjall and Hafrafell across Skaftafellsjökull in the south
Back Cover Photograph: Hraunfossar and the river Hvítá in the west
Page 1 Photograph: Rooftop, Downtown Reykjavík
Page 3 Photograph: Strokkur at Haukadalur in the south-west
Page 112 Photograph: Atlantic Puffin

ICELAND

COLIN BAXTER

Introduction by Cathy Harlow

Colin Baxter Photography, Grantown-on-Spey, Scotland

ICELAND

Icelanders bond so tenaciously with their homeland or *heim*, that they can seldom stay away long without succumbing to melancholy and nostalgia. Far from blind patriotism, it is the collective memory of 1100 years of history, and of the hardship and heroics that are inextricably a part of it. Some chapters are so well documented that people can credibly trace their lineage back to ninth-century Norway and the age of expansion in Europe, which prompted the Viking raids on Britain as well as the settlement of Iceland. Overpopulation and rivalry among Norway's struggling petty kingdoms had left many families landless, provoking one of the greatest sea migrations of all time. As well as the catalyst, Norway, with its skills of ship building, navigation and seamanship, could provide the means. Possibly as many as 25,000 people in search of a new life made the epic voyage over the North Atlantic to land on Iceland's windblown shores. Over a 50-year period, the incipient island nation emerged and went on to discover Greenland and North America.

Iceland's settlement was no accidental journey into the unknown; Norseman Hrafna-Flóki had attempted to settle there some years earlier. Finding the fishing so good, he neglected to make hay for his livestock and over the winter they perished. Before leaving in the spring, he climbed a mountain and saw a fjord filled with drift ice. Disgruntled, he is credited with giving the island its uninviting name – Ísland, meaning 'ice land'. The title of the first official settler was, however, awarded to one Ingólfur Arnarson, who around the year 874 arrived to claim a bay where billowing steam was seen rising from the land. He named it Reykjavík, 'smoke bay', by coincidence the very site where Iceland's capital city stands today.

The new arrivals found that the island, a little larger than Ireland in size, was uninhabited. Every patch of suitable land was parcelled out by the year 930, a historic landmark when the renowned legislative and judicial body, the Althing, was founded at a place called Þingvellir. The island's coastal plains and lush valleys were now fully settled, but further inland, beyond the fringes of the habitable world, lay a sparsely vegetated highland plateau, punctuated by huge ice fields and precipitous mountain ranges.

This no man's land became a place of refuge for fugitives and outlaws, banished there by the law courts at Þingvellir. The threads of their story and that of Iceland's other early settlers form the fabric of the celebrated Icelandic sagas. Literary masterpieces that are an enigmatic blend of medieval fact and fiction, the sagas tell of family feuds and vengeance, heinous crimes and punishments, liberally embellished with illuminating glimpses of life at the time they were written. For Icelanders, the manuscripts are a priceless national treasure and hugely symbolic, their fate appearing to mirror that of the nation. By the end of the fourteenth century, when the last of them were laboriously being inscribed on vellum, Iceland had already ceded its legislative authority to Norway, and was about to join a union under the Danish Crown. By 1702, when Icelandic scholar Árni Magnússon was commissioned to carry out a census of his country, over three hundred years of colonial oppression, epidemics and natural disasters had left the economy in ruins and the morale of its people at rock bottom. Árni's personal crusade, as he travelled from farm to farm, was to hunt out the treasured manuscripts and remove them to Denmark where they remained in exile for 250 years.

Following independence from Denmark in 1918, and the formation of the Republic in 1944, a further 27 years passed before the first of the sagas returned home. In an unprecedented move, the Danish government agreed to hand back to its former colony many of the manuscripts,

Herðubreið from Askja in the Highlands

Þingvellir – Seat of Iceland´s original Parliament in the south-west

including the precious *Flateyjarbók* and *Konungsbók*, whose pages chronicled episodes of Scandinavian history as well as that of Iceland. With no great architectural heritage to speak of, these volumes embodied the spirit of the Icelandic nation so it was little wonder that the event aroused such intense national pride. Even today, books are the most worthy of gifts and Icelanders read more, borrow more books from libraries and publish more works per head of population, than most other nations in the world. Incredibly, the Icelandic language survived the influences of centuries of Danish colonisation. What is spoken today is changed remarkably little from that of the sagas, a grammatically complex yet hugely expressive tongue, so pure that any new adopted word must await official approval. The land described so vividly in the sagas is as recognisable and real today as 800 years ago, giving Icelanders a very tangible link with their past and origins. Place names are unchanged, farms still occupy the same site and the mountains cast the same long shadows in winter, from a sun which reluctantly hovers over the horizon for an hour or two.

Lying just south of the Arctic Circle, Iceland escapes the polar night so there are always several hours of daylight even in the darkest months from November to February. This is the time when the spectacular *aurora borealis* is most often seen, its rippling curtains of coloured light dancing across a cloudless night sky. In summer, by contrast, there is no darkness from May to early August. For a week or so in June, the sun doesn't fully set, but caresses the arctic horizon for about an hour, letting one day merge into another. In spite of its name, Iceland rarely gets the extreme cold usual at this latitude, while summer temperatures average a pleasant 11°C. Such a narrow range is typical of a temperate oceanic climate, the most apt way of describing Iceland's weather. The prevailing southerly winds dump their moisture-laden cargo high on the summits of the southern half of the island. In winter, this falls as snow, accumulating to form vast dome-shaped

ice fields, that the Icelanders call *jökull*. The largest, mighty Vatnajökull covers 8300 sq km and is over a kilometre thick in places. Spilling down at its fringe are numerous glaciers, their gaping crevasses as formidable an obstacle as the murky melt water that leaks from their snouts to form Iceland's largest rivers. Unpredictable and unruly and forever changing course, their flow can treble in a matter of hours following a warm or wet spell. Only after a volcanic eruption under the ice are they at their most threatening, swelling to a volume equal to the flow of the Amazon at its mouth, an unstoppable force that can carry off icebergs the size of houses.

Icelanders have learned to live with such disasters, their civil defence force equipped to meet not the threat of invasion or war but that of nature. That said, it is hard to imagine that anything could have halted the destructive force of Laki, a 1783 eruption that dumped lava on 565 sq km of farmland, emitting a cloud of sulphur dioxide and other noxious gases that enveloped the island in a lethal bluish haze. Toxic fluorine, leached from the millions of tons of falling ash, killed the livestock, and in the famine that followed one fifth of Iceland's population died. Fortunately for Iceland such cataclysmic events are rare, though volcanic eruptions are not, occurring on average every three years.

To blame for this jittery state of affairs is Iceland's location astride the mid-Atlantic ridge, a tectonic plate boundary that runs the length of the Atlantic. As the plates drift apart, the wound in the crust fills with new material forced up from the earth's mantle. At several points along the rift, volcanic island clusters have formed, but none come close to matching Iceland in size. Here, the process is ongoing and where the rift cuts through the centre from south west to north east, the country is growing at a rate of about one centimetre a year. All of this makes Iceland's rocks volcanic in origin, but what is more astonishing is that they are so young. While some of neighbouring Greenland's mountains are 4600 million years

Viking ship sculpture 'Sólfar' by Jón Gunnar Árnason, Rauðarárvík, Reykjavík

old and among the most ancient on earth, the contents of Iceland's showcase of geological curiosities are all younger than 16 million years. Few places can rival the island for its variety of volcanic features, among them pseudo craters, tephra rings, lava tubes and shield volcanoes – names as exotic and colourful as the scenery they create.

When the Ice Age set in three million years ago, the volcanoes kept on erupting, melting huge cavities which filled with new rock under the kilometre-thick ice sheets. After the last great thaw, 10,000 years ago, the land had changed beyond recognition and great mountain ranges had grown from the sub-glacial eruptions. Composed mainly of crumbly textured rocks, like easily eroded tuff and rhyolite, they are the riotously coloured mountains at Landmannalaugar, the gorges and moss-clad cliffs of Þórsmörk and the great grey ridges that transect the northern desert. Where the eruptions were long and concentrated, they broke through the ice and a hard cap of lava formed. After it melted, flat-topped 'table' mountains with precipitous sides were left behind, of which shapely Herðubreið, known to Icelanders as 'Queen of the mountains', is the most striking. With landscapes like these, it is small wonder that the country's rich folklore has produced such a wealth of elemental beings. The most odious are the trolls, though there is little to fear from those turned to stone by the rays of the sun, now silhouetted on the slopes of the hills or in among the lava flows.

The older landscapes of the east, north and north-west of the island were chipped, scraped and sculpted into fjords and steep-sided valleys for many thousands of years. Bizarre stepped patterns are the hallmark of their mountains, each layer a sheet basalt from the forceful eruptions that built the foundations of the island. In many places, there is little point in farming – there simply isn't enough land – but the sheltered fjords offer safe, deep-water harbours for trawlers. Conveniently, the warm and cold ocean currents around Iceland mingle to create ideal spawning conditions for several valuable fish species. Brightly painted houses strung out along the shores of the fjord form close-knit, self-sufficient communities that for almost a hundred years had processed the bulk of a catch amounting to three-quarters of the nation's export earnings. In an effort to sustainably manage fish stocks, quotas, enforced by the government, now limit the catch for each vessel. Such action was taken to ensure the long-term future of the fishing industry in Iceland.

In recent decades, people have moved to the towns and the capital for a better choice of job. This shift in population from the villages to the city is often attributed to a decline in the fishing industry. This, however, is a misconception. The fishing industry, far from being a failing enterprise, still constitutes 70 per cent of the country's exports. It generates a great amount of revenue and represents a stable source of income for the nation. The steady movement of the population to the towns and cities is attributable to people wanting to maintain a higher standard of living. In a country where 98 per cent of the population are employed and earning comparatively high wages, it is not a suprising trend. However, addressing the problem of depopulation is one item on a long agenda of pressing issues facing the government and its people.

Another urgent need is that of conservation and the protection of what is now being recognised as one of Iceland's greatest assets – its vast tracts of uninhabited wilderness, a region of extraordinary natural beauty that makes up about half of the country's surface area. Iceland has a credible environmental track record, helped by the lack of any obviously exploitable mineral deposits, though sulphur and calcite were once mined. Apart from a ferro-silicon plant, an aluminium factory and a cement works, heavy industry is virtually absent and the island's air and water are about as pure as they come. Roughly 80 per cent of homes, offices and factories, particularly in and around the capital, are heated from geothermal bores,

Jökulsárlón and Breiðamerkurjökull in the south-east

by tapping into the hot springs and steam vents that are a characteristic feature of the landscape. Almost all electricity is generated by hydroelectric schemes, harnessing the country's powerful rivers so efficiently that further projects are planned and there are schemes afoot to sell off the surplus to foreign investors. While no one disputes the need to reduce dependence on fishing, the large scale flooding of pristine wilderness may yet prove to be Iceland's most contentious issue.

The largest tract of this fragile asset lies in a rain shadow north of the ice caps, encompassing the bleak but evocative Sprengisandur desert and legendary Ódáðahraun lava fields. Also at stake is the wilderness lying east and west of the mighty Jökulsá á Fjöllum. This powerful river boasts a trio of awesome waterfalls on its journey north to the Arctic Ocean, including 45m high Dettifoss, Iceland's most powerful.

The climate north of the ice caps is drier and the landscape apparently barren except along the banks of freshwater streams, where luminous green moss, stands of angelica and clumps of bright purple arctic river beauty break up the sea of grey. But looking closer, you find dozens of plants that positively thrive in this bleakest of habitats: heads of pin-cushion like moss campion, whose foot-long tap root ensures its survival; great clumps of thrift and sea campion, coastal plants that are out of place, yet totally at home in Iceland's inland desert.

A staggering half of Iceland is desert; 11% is ice covered; 3% is made up of lakes and ponds while 10% has gone under lava in the last 10,000 years. Just 1% is cultivated, producing silage to feed several hundred thousand sheep, horses and cattle over the winter. This leaves only one quarter of the country with continuous vegetation cover. Early accounts suggest that when the island was first settled, half of it was suitable for grazing and at least a fifth may have supported a forest of dwarf birch, willow and rowan. If there is one thing about the country that is glaringly obvious today, it is the absence of trees. Cut by the early settlers for fuel, when the climate worsened the forests could not recover. Also to blame are the sheep, brought in and allowed to roam where no animal had grazed before. Their tender spring buds nipped off, the trees simply couldn't survive. The disappearance of the forests has been linked to the devastating soil erosion that, if not checked, would leave Iceland scarcely habitable. As if to prove the point, where pockets of forest and grassland have been fenced off from sheep, their recovery has taken just a few years.

Compared to other sub-arctic lands, Iceland has very few wild animals because of its isolation since the end of the Ice Age. Only one land mammal found today, the arctic fox, was there at the time of settlement. Introduced mice, rats, mink and reindeer have successfully adapted to a feral existence, while descendants of the farm animals brought in by the early settlers are now recognised as distinct breeds. The hardy and sure-footed Icelandic horse, for centuries the only means of transport over the island's rugged terrain, has a special gait, the *tölt*, a very fast yet smooth trot which lets the rider cover long distances at speed and in comfort.

Iceland has long been acclaimed as a key bird-watching location. The Lake Mývatn area in the north-east, is known for its abundant wildfowl. More than 14 species of ducks breed in and around the lake and its surrounding rivers and ponds. Species such as the red-breasted merganser, long-tailed duck, Barrow's goldeneye and the harlequin duck are sighted regularly. Iceland is the only European breeding ground for the Barrow's goldeneye. Though by no means common, the impressive great northern diver can be seen on lakes and fjords, particularly in the north. With the advantage of flight, birds can easily colonise and in the last hundred years, eight new species have established themselves in Iceland, to give a total of over 70 breeding birds. While this is a rather meagre total, some, like puffins, guillemots and kittiwakes, are found in vast numbers, their nesting sites using every available burrow and ledge on the dizzy heights of the island's coastal cliffs. People used to lower themselves down the cliffs by rope to collect the birds and their eggs, which provided a welcome change from a diet of fish and lamb. Nowadays, the eggs are more of a delicacy than a supplementary necessity and can be purchased in many supermarkets throughout the country.

Though sheep farming was for centuries the mainstay of the economy, the sea has always been a dominant force in people's lives – most Icelanders live within 10 kilometres of the coast – and many are only too familiar with its whims. Practically every coastal village and town has a poignant memorial to its missing and dead. While Iceland is now a leader in the design and production of safety and rescue equipment and clothing, this is little consolation to the families of those who have lost their lives.

Offshore, the rich coastal waters attract not only fish, but also abundant marine mammals, and Iceland is gaining a reputation as a major whale-watching destination. Following man's virtual extermination of blue whales in the southern hemisphere, to quietly observe a whale the size of a jumbo jet and the largest animal ever to have lived, seems a privilege that few would believe possible. Yet these gentle giants, along with humpback, minke, fin and sei whales, orcas and many species of dolphins form an impressive list of cetaceans that are regularly sighted off Iceland, to the delight of whale watchers. This is one reason why tourism figures have doubled in the last 10 years. Another is the pervading feeling of space and room to breathe that anyone coming from overcrowded, traffic-choked Europe or North America cannot help but sense.

With stunning scenery everywhere, you might wonder why almost two thirds of the population of 280,000 live in just one corner of the island, in and around the capital Reykjavík – especially puzzling since until a hundred years ago or so, there were no towns, nor barely any villages in Iceland.

More jobs, a better education and the lure of city life are the obvious answers, but there is more to it. For centuries, the entirely rural Icelanders had struggled with nature and isolation, knowing none of the refinements and culture of the rest of Europe – for example, only in 1974 was the circular route around the island completed and the last of the glacial rivers bridged. Icelanders crave material comforts and gadgetry in a curious mix of obsession, naivety and good taste. Yet the same high-tech home may have treasured original paintings on the wall. With the often harsh weather and long winter nights, they can be forgiven for lavishing money and attention on the home. But it doesn't end here; the city's streets and parks are a sculpture gallery, there are several professional theatre companies, numerous galleries and museums, an opera, symphony orchestra, university and lively pop music scene. Icelandic footballers have for years fed the league teams of Europe and all of this from a population that scarcely equals that of a very average European or North American town.

Each year on December 31st Iceland sits down to watch the national television station's parody of the events of the year, a chance for the whole nation to unite in the humour and joy of being Icelandic, in a way that no foreigner could truly understand. Then, the ritual over, they spill on to the streets to bring in the New Year and let rip with a firework display that is unmatched in its spontaneity, intensity and anarchy.

Beneath a veneer of material success, modern Icelandic culture is intriguing and magnetic in its appeal. It is a classless society, where everyone is comfortable on first name terms and young and old are at ease with one another. Visitors may be first drawn by Iceland´s landscapes, yet they are soon infected by the effervescence of its youthful culture and experience a kind of rejuvenation, a process of re-energising that is at once therapeutic and highly addictive.

Cathy Harlow

New Year firework celebrations and the floodlit Hallgrímkirkja, Reykjavík

The Blue Lagoon, Reykjanes *(opposite)*
Blesi at Haukadalur in the south-west *(right)*

Ófærufoss in the southern Highlands –
the natural arch collapsed in 1993

Hvítserkur and Húnafjörður in the north-west

Suðurdalur and Asunnarstaðafell at Breiðdalur, Eastern Fjords

Landmannalaugar in the southern Highlands

Vattarfjörður, Skálmarnesmúlafjall and Kerlingarfjörður, Western Fjords

Bustarfell Folk Museum, Hofsárdalur, Vopnafjörður in the north-east

21

Dyngjufjöll across Vikursandur, Highlands

Látrabjarg and Bæjarbjarg, Western Fjords

Goðafoss – 'Falls of the Gods' in the north *(above)*
Drangahraun and Svartahraun below Snæfellsjökull, Snæfellsnes *(opposite)*

Stigárjökull and Bleikafjall in the south-east *(opposite)*
Eskifjorður, Eastern Fjords *(above)*

Víti and Öskjuvatn at Askja in the Highlands

28

Kleifarvatn and Sveifluháls near Hafnarfjörður in the south-west

Snæfellsjökull across Breiðafjörður in the west

Geitlandsjökull and Þórisjökull from Kaldidalur in the western Highlands

Gullfoss – 'The Golden Falls' in the south-west

Breiðavik, Western Fjords

Vigur and Snæfjallaströnd, Ísafjarðardjúp, Western Fjords

Stóhöfði, southern Highlands

Stykkishólmur, Snæfellsnes

36

Strokkur at Haukadalur in the south-west

Látrabjarg from Bjargtangar –
'the westernmost point in Europe',
Western Fjords *(left)*
Barðaströnd, Western Fjords *(opposite)*

Drangey, Málmey and Þórðarhöfði, Skagafjorður from Sauðárkrókur in the north *(opposite)*
Böggvisstaðafjall, Eyjafjörður and Hrísey from Latraströnd in the north *(above)*

41

Kviárjökull in the south-east

Laxárdalur near Mývatn in the north-east

Rauðisandur, Western Fjords

Kögur, Hornstrandir

Geysir at Haukadalur in the south-west *(above)*
Staðarstaður and Langavatn, Snæfellsnes *(opposite)*

Hellutindur and Múlahyrna below Öræfajökull in the south *(opposite)*
Víknafjöll across Skjálfandi near Húsavík in the north-east *(above)*

Dettifoss in the north-east

Jökulsárgljúfur in the north-east

Seljalandsfoss in the south *(above)*
Hrútárjökull and Fjallsjökull across Jökulsárlón in the south-east *(opposite)*

Langjökull from Svartárbugur, Highlands *(opposite)*
Kerlingarfjöll, Highlands *(above)*

Geothermal area at Kerlingarfjöll in the Highlands

Reyðarfjörður, Eastern Fjords

Kirkjuból across Dýrafjörður in the Western Fjords

Bólstaðarhlíð, Svartárdalur in the north

59

Aldeyjarfoss in the northern Highlands

Króksbjarg, Skagaströnd and Húnaflói in the north-west

61

Arnarstapi Harbour, Breiðavik, Snæfellsnes

62

Snæfellsjökull across Búðavik, Snæfellsnes

Lómagnúpur and Oræfajökull in the south

Jökulsárlon glacial lagoon in the south-east

Eyrarfjall, Sauðdalsfell and Kambfjall across Reyðarfjörður, Eastern Fjords

Dynjandi, Western Fjords

Humpback Whale near Húsavík, Skjálfandi in the north-east *(above)*
Ingólfshöfði in the south-east *(opposite)*

Reykjaströnd and Skagafjöður in the north *(opposite)*
Hverfjall at Mývatn in the north-east *(above)*

Grænahlið, Ísafjarðardjúp, Western Fjords

Kinnafjöll from Fljótsheiði in the north

73

Elliðaey, Vestmannaeyjar and Eyjafjallajökull

Súlnasker, Geldungur, Hellisey and Suðurey, Vestmannaeyjar

Buðlungaflói and Mývatn from Vindbelgjarfjall in the north-east

Geothermal area at Námafjall near Mývatn

Vestrahorn near Höfn in the south-east

Vatnajökull and Höfn from across Skarðsfjörður in the south-east

Norðurbarmur, Landmannalaugar in the southern Highlands *(above)*
Innstihaus, Kirkjuhaus, and Mosahaus below the northern side of Eyjafjallajökull in the south *(opposite)*

Þorgeirsfell, Snæfellsnes *(opposite)*
Háifoss in the south-west *(right)*

Sölvanöf, Melrakkaslétta in the north-east

Ísafjörður, Ísafjarðardjúp and Snæfjallaströnd, Western Fjords

Svínafellsjökull near Skaftafell in the south

Bárðarbunga, Vatnajökull in the Highlands

Víti at Krafla near Mývatn in the north-east *(above)*
Hveradalur, Kverkfjöll in the eastern Highlands *(opposite)*

Snæfell from Hrafnkelsdalur,
eastern Highlands *(opposite)*
Skógafoss in the south *(right)*

Volcanic eruption beneath Vatnajökull in 1996

Mávabyggðir and Breiðamerkurjökull across Jökulsárlón

Herðubreið across Krepputunga, Highlands

94

Hvalfjörður in the south-west

Langadalsfjall, Þingeyrasandur and Húnafjörður in the north-west

Skálatindur near Höfn in the south-east

Álftafjörður and Melrakkanes, Eastern Fjords *(above)*
Búrfell from Námafjall by Mývatn in the north-east *(opposite)*

Miðaftanstindur and Fjallsjökull across Fjallsárlón in the south-east *(opposite)*
Towards Hverfjall from Neslandatangi, Mývatn *(above)*

Hallgrímkirkja, Reykjavík

Höfði, Reykjavík –
The 1986 Reagan / Gorbachev summit venue

Arnardrangur and Reynisdrangar
from Dyrhólaey – the southernmost
point of the mainland

Vatnsfjorður and Breiðafjörður from Fossá, Western Fjords

Strokkur at Haukadalur in the south-west *(above)*
Vestmannaeyjar from Landeyjasandur in the south *(opposite)*

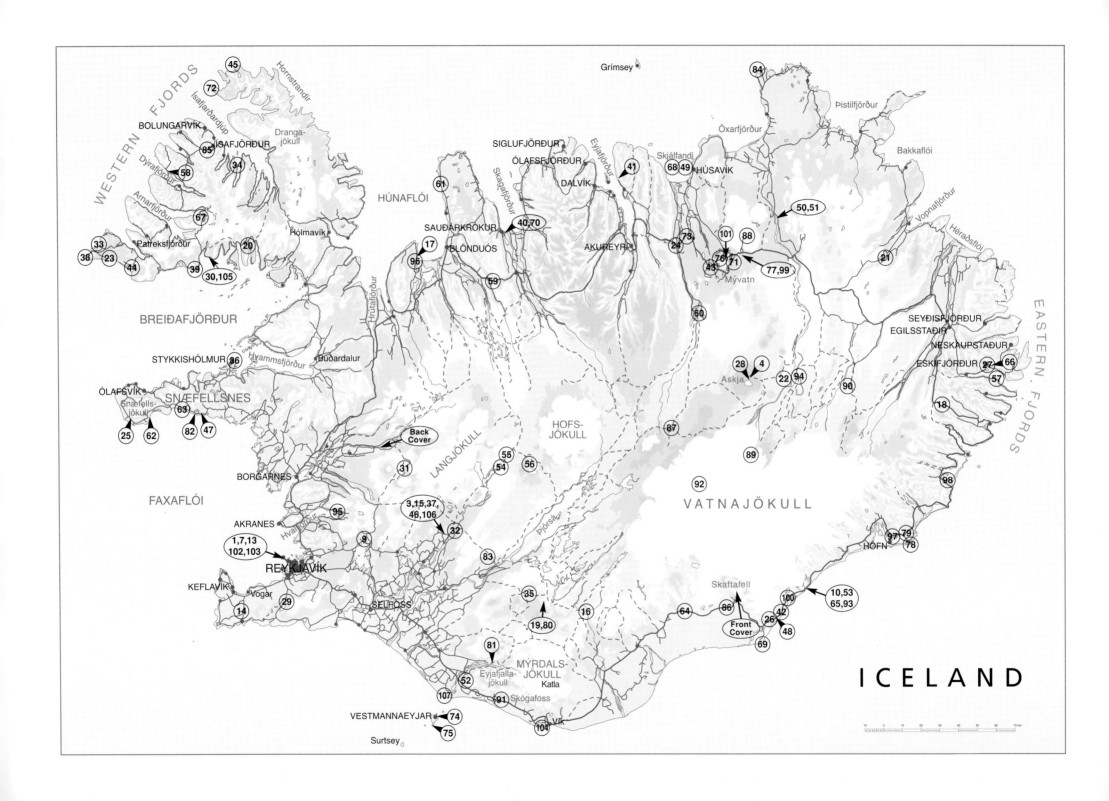

ICELAND

INDEX OF PLACES

Listed in order of page number

Front Cover: Öræfajökull, Hrútsfjall and Hafrafell

Back Cover: Hraunfossar and the river Hvítá

The page numbers on the map opposite indicate the position from where each photograph was taken.

INFORMATION ABOUT ICELAND

Geography

Position: North Atlantic island, whose northernmost peninsula extends to just three kilometres short of the Arctic Circle.

Nearest Neighbours: Greenland (287 km), Scotland (798 km) and Norway (970 km).

Ocean Currents: the warm Gulf Stream and cold east Greenland current mingle off Iceland's west coast. Both affect the climate. Where the currents meet, an upwelling of nutrient-rich water attracts fish and a variety of marine mammals.

Coastline: total length: 4970 km

Offshore Islands: numerous uninhabited islands, mostly formed by submarine eruptions. The Westman Islands (Vestmannaeyjar) off the south coast, Grímsey and Hrísey in the north and Flatey in the west are inhabited.

Area: 103,000 sq km of which 12% glaciers and ice caps; 3% lakes; 10% post-Ice Age lava flows; 25% continuous vegetation; 1% cultivated land; 1% forested.

Ice Caps: Vatnajökull (8300 sq km); Langjökull (950 sq km); Hofsjökull (925 sq km); Mýrdalsjökull (596 sq km).

Highest Mountain: Hvannadalshnúkur (2119m) on Öræfajökull, which is an active strata volcano on the Vatnajökull massif.

Highest Free-Standing Peaks: Snæfell (1833m) a strato volcano and Herðubreið (1682m) a 'table' mountain formed under ice during the Ice Age.

Largest Lake: Þingvallavatn (87 sq km), formed by tectonic subsidence.

Deepest Lake: Öskjuvatn (220 m), formed by subsidence following the collapse of a magma chamber under the Askja volcano.

Volcanoes

Hekla: a ridge volcano formed in the last 8800 years and among the most active in Iceland. A major eruption in 1104 buried many farms under ash; another in 1947 lasted 13 months. Smaller eruptions in 1970, 1980/1981, 1991 and 2000. Loss of life, as a consequence of volcanic activity, is virtually unheard of in the twentieth century.

Katla: located under the ice cap Mýrdalsjökull, Katla is active roughly every 50 years and last erupted in 1918. Eruptions are accompanied by catastrophic glacial bursts of melt water.

Grímsvötn / Bárðarbunga: volcanic system under the ice cap Vatnajökull, which erupts at 10-20 year intervals. A major eruption in 1996 was followed by huge floods, dumping four cubic kilometres of water and a million tons of ice on the outwash plain to its south.

Laki: a single eruption in 1783 that ranks among the greatest and most damaging in historical times.

Krafla: the most active volcano in the north of Iceland, located by Lake Mývatn, whose people suffered greatly during the 1724-1728 eruptions. More recently there were 11 small eruptions from 1975-1984.

Askja: a major volcanic system with a prominent lake-filled caldera, lying in the heart of Iceland's northern desert. Ash falls from the eruption of 1875 destroyed grazing lands and prompted the emigration of Icelanders to North America. Most recently it erupted in 1961.

Öræfajökull: Iceland's highest mountain and volcano has erupted twice since the settlement, in 1362, when around 40 farms were destroyed, and again in 1727.

Vestmannaeyjar: offshore island group formed in submarine eruptions over the last 8000 years. The youngest island, Surtsey, formed in eruptions from 1963-1967, while in 1973, an eruption on Heimaey destroyed 40% of the houses in Iceland's most important fishing town. Fortunately, all inhabitants were safely brought to the mainland on fishing boats on the first night.

National Parks and Protected Areas

Þingvellir National Park: historic assembly site of the Althing, with varied bird life and flora and many geological features.

Jökulságljúfur National Park: centred on the rugged gorges carved out by the glacial Jökulsá river. The park has stunning eroded volcanic plugs, basalt columns, pockets of lush birch forest and many exceptional waterfalls.

Skaftafell National Park: awesome glaciers and mountain scenery, waterfalls and pleasant woodland.

Fjallabak Nature Reserve: colourful rhyolite mountainous region centred on Landmannalaugar, with hot springs, craters and moss-clad hills.

Hornstrandir Nature Reserve: an uninhabited region of fjords and glaciated mountains in the far north-west. Prolific bird life and wildflowers, good chances of seeing arctic foxes, and adventurous hiking.

Lake Mývatn Conservation Area: among Iceland's best-known areas of natural beauty, with abundant volcanic features, geothermal activity and huge numbers of breeding ducks.

Herðubreiðarlindir Nature Reserve & Askja: fragile desert 'oasis' at the foot of shapely Mt. Herðubreið in the central highlands, where a surprising number of birds and plants thrive. The moonscapes of Askja were used to train NASA astronauts.

People

Origin: descended from Norse settlers in the ninth century, some arriving via the northern British Isles. Their Irish slaves account for a Celtic element in the bloodline.

Population of Iceland: 280,000, of which almost two thirds live in the south-west.

Reykjavík: capital city with 110,000 (39% of the population).

Akureyri (north): 15,000 and the largest town outside the capital area.

Other Regional Centres: Ísafjörður (north-west) 2900; Egilsstaðir (east) 1600; Höfn (south-east) 1800.

Population Density: 2.6 inhabitants per sq km makes Iceland by far the most sparsely inhabited country in Europe.

Society

Iceland is a welfare state, whose people are a highly educated and literate nation. Education is free, up to and including university, as is hospital treatment, though a small charge is made to visit a doctor. Family ties are strong and people make a special effort to be together at Christmas and other important occasions. A system of patronyms is used instead of surnames and everyone is on first name terms.

Government

An independent republic since 1944, Iceland is a parliamentary democracy with an elected president as head of state and a prime minister and cabinet in government. A parliament of 63 members is elected on a proportional representation basis. Nearly all governments since independence have been coalitions.

Economy

Exports: based on fish with a total catch of around two million tons a year. Cod, quick frozen in factories around the island, is the most valuable species, while flatfish, redfish, shrimp, herring and capelin are also significant.

Other Industrial Output: includes aluminium, ferro-silicon and diatomite. Smaller manufacturing outlets produce soft drinks, plastics, clothing, footwear and foodstuffs. Life-saving equipment and clothing for seamen, computerised weighing scales, geothermal technology and computer software are developing sectors.

Agriculture: accounts for less than 2% of export earnings but Iceland is self-sufficient in meat and dairy produce. Potatoes and turnips can be sown outdoors, while geothermally heated glasshouses grow tomatoes, cucumbers, peppers, indoor plants and cut flowers.

Imports: include food, consumer goods, vehicles, fuel and industrial raw materials.

Employment: agriculture: 4%; fishing & fish processing: 10%; manufacturing: 12%; services: 66%.

Unemployment: 2%-4% in recent years.

Trading Partners: EU countries account for around 70% of imports and exports, the USA around 10% and the Far East and other countries about 20%.

Iceland enjoys one of the highest GNP (per capita) in the world.

Flora & Fauna

Flora: around 450 flowering plants and many hundreds of colourful fungi, lichens and mosses. 97% of plants are also found in Norway but very few are of North American origin.

Birds: around 70 species regularly breed. Others are passage migrants or accidental visitors. Sea birds, waders and wildfowl are most common.

Mammals: arctic foxes are common but elusive. Also found are introduced mink, reindeer, mice and rats. Harbour and grey seals are common. Minke whales, humpback whales, blue whales, fin whales, sei whales and sperm whales inhabit offshore and coastal waters, along with pilot whales, orcas, white-beaked dolphins, white-sided dolphins and harbour porpoises.

Weather

Average Reykjavík Temperatures: -1°C (January); +11°C (July).

Colder temperatures are experienced in the north and east of the country in winter and can drop to –20°C. In summer it is often warmer in the north and east (+20°C is not uncommon) and usually drier.

Rainfall: highest in the south and west with an average of 1600 mm per year.

Winds: a completely calm day is unusual. Strong winds can be expected at any time of year. Northerly winds bring rain to the north but fine weather to the south while southerly winds do the reverse. In theory, therefore, there is usually somewhere on the island with good weather.

Travelling to Iceland

The national airline Icelandair flies daily to several North American and European destinations. Iceland is a popular stopover on transatlantic flights. There is also a ferry service in summer linking Seyðisfjöður with the Faroes, Norway, Denmark and Shetland.

Getting Around

Public Transport: domestic air and bus services link towns and villages but there are no railways.

By Car: a 1400 km circular route, now mostly paved, makes it possible to drive around Iceland in a matter of days, but a week or two is needed to do the country justice and explore side roads. Dirt tracks and gravel roads, often with unbridged rivers, criss-cross the uninhabited highlands, for which high-clearance four-wheel drive vehicles are almost always needed. Car hire is available.

When to Visit

Warmest Months: June, July & August.

Birds: late May to early July.

Flowers: mid June and July.

Whales: June, July and August (trips also run May & September but may be colder and rougher seas).

Scenery: any time of year but the landscape is at its most colourful in summer.

Northern Lights: end of August to March but luck plays a big part.

Visitor Facilities

Accommodation: hotels and guesthouses in the capital, other towns and country areas. Farm guesthouses offer a mix of hotel and hostel style accommodation. Not all accommodation is open from September to May.

Campsites: in towns, villages, national parks and conservation areas.

Activities: horse riding, whale-watching, walking, sightseeing, flights, boat and coach excursions, bird-watching, snowmobiling and cross-country skiing.

Attractions: many interesting museums in the capital and around the island – not all are open September to May.

Festivals

New Year's Eve: one of the world's best spontaneous firework shows takes place around midnight in the capital.

Þorrablót (at various times in February): a feast of pagan origins, when people gather to eat traditional foods like smoked lamb, rotten shark and singed sheep head, accompanied by music, singing, drinking and story-telling.

First Day of Summer: a public holiday, usually celebrated on the third Thursday in April.

Seamen's Day: celebrated on the first Sunday in June in the fishing villages, with light-hearted festivities and competitions.

Independence Day: on 17th June, celebrations are held around the country, with the liveliest in the capital.

Verslunarmannahelgi: the first weekend in August is a long holiday weekend. Special events and celebrations are held around the island.

Réttadagur: in September, farmers celebrate the sheep round-up with song, dance and merry-making.

Christmas: in the build up to Christmas, the 13 capricious Christmas Lads come down from the mountains to make mischief but bring small gifts to lucky children and leave their shoes in the window. Christmas itself is a quiet family occasion, celebrated with a festive dinner and exchange of gifts on the evening of 24th December.